PEAK PERFORMANCE PLATES: A NUTRITIONIST'S GUIDE TO HIGH ALTITUDE EATING

A HANDBOOK ON HIGH ALTITUDE NUTRITION

BIJOYA BHATTACHARJEE

Made with ♥ on the Notion Press Platform
www.notionpress.com

DEDICATION

To the pillars of my life and this endeavor:

In loving memory of my mother, Late Shikha Bhattacharjee, whose nurturing spirit continues to guide me.

To my father, Mr. Bhabani Pada Bhattacharjee, for his enduring strength and encouragement.

To my uncle, Dr. Prodip Bhattacharjee, for his wisdom and steadfast support.

To my beloved sisters, Bidula Bhattacharjee and Biproja Bhattacharjee, for their constant love and unwavering belief in me.

Your collective faith and support have been my sustenance, much like the nutrition this book aims to provide. Your influence reaches the highest altitudes of my heart, just as this guide aspires to nourish those who climb great heights.

This work stands as a testament to the love and support of my entire family, who have always lifted me up.

Contents

Foreword

The human body is a marvel of adaptation, capable of surviving and even thriving in the most challenging environments on Earth. Yet, as we ascend to great heights, we push our physiology to its limits. The rarefied air of high altitudes presents unique challenges to our bodies, affecting everything from our respiratory system to our digestion and metabolism.

In this crucial intersection of extreme environments and human physiology, nutrition plays a pivotal role. The food we consume becomes not just sustenance, but a powerful tool for adaptation, performance, and survival. This is where "Peak Performance Plates" steps in, offering a comprehensive guide to navigating the complex world of high-altitude nutrition.

As a nutritionist with years of experience working with mountaineers, altitude researchers, and high-altitude expedition teams, the author brings a wealth of practical knowledge and scientific understanding to this often-overlooked aspect of altitude preparation. This book bridges the gap between cutting-edge nutritional science and real-world application in extreme conditions.

Within these pages, you'll find not just theory, but practical advice on meal planning, nutrient timing, and food selection tailored specifically for high-altitude environments. Whether you're a seasoned mountaineer, a trekking enthusiast, or a support team member for high-altitude expeditions, this guide will equip you with the nutritional knowledge to optimize your performance and well-being at elevation.

"Peak Performance Plates" is more than just a nutrition manual; it's a key to unlocking your body's potential in one of Earth's most challenging environments. As you embark on your high-altitude adventures, let this book be your trusted companion in fueling your journey to the top.

Wishing you safe climbs and nutritious meals at every altitude,

Bijoya Bhattacharjee

Assistant Professor - Department of Dietetics and Applied Nutrition, Amity University Kolkata

Founder and Consultant Dietitian - Clinical Nutrition and Wellness Solutions (CNWS)

Ph.D Scholar, M.Sc Community Nutrition and Dietetics Management, Certified FODMAP Dietitian, CDE, LLL Certified from ESPEN, B,Sc Clinical

Nutrition and Dietetics

Preface

Welcome to "Peak Performance Plates: A Nutritionist's Guide to High Altitude Eating". This book is designed to equip mountaineers, trekkers, and high-altitude adventurers with the knowledge and strategies needed to optimize their nutritional approach in oxygen-scarce environments.

The challenges of high-altitude environments extend far beyond the physical demands of ascending steep terrain. As we climb higher, our bodies face a complex array of physiological changes that significantly impact our nutritional needs. The air becomes thinner, our metabolisms shift, and even the simple act of digestion can become more challenging.

In this guide, we delve deep into the science of high-altitude nutrition, translating complex physiological concepts into practical, actionable advice. From understanding the increased caloric demands at altitude to balancing macronutrients for optimal performance, we cover all aspects of fueling your body in the mountains.

You'll learn about the crucial role of hydration at altitude, strategies for maintaining electrolyte balance, and how to combat the appetite suppression often experienced at high elevations. We'll explore the importance of key nutrients in supporting acclimatization and discuss how to plan and prepare meals that are not only nutritious but also practical for high-altitude expeditions.

Whether you're planning your first high-altitude trek or you're a seasoned mountaineer looking to refine your nutritional strategy, this guide offers valuable insights to enhance your performance, safety, and enjoyment in the world's highest places.

Remember, proper nutrition is not just about fueling your body—it's a critical component of acclimatization, risk management, and overall well-being at altitude. By mastering the principles outlined in this guide, you'll be better prepared to meet the unique challenges of high-altitude environments and fully embrace the incredible experiences they offer.

So, as you prepare to ascend to new heights, let this guide be your companion in ensuring that your body is as well-prepared as your mind and gear. Here's to safe, successful, and well-fueled adventures in the high places of the world!

Acknowledgements

This book would not have been possible without the support, guidance, and inspiration of many individuals. I would like to express my deepest gratitude to:

My family, the bedrock of my life and career, in loving memory of my mother, Late Shikha Bhattacharjee, whose nurturing spirit continues to guide me, my father, Mr. Bhabani Pada Bhattacharjee, for his unwavering support and encouragement, my uncle, Dr. Prodip Bhattacharjee, for his wisdom and steadfast guidance, my beloved sisters, Bidula Bhattacharjee and Biproja Bhattacharjee, for their constant love and belief in me.

My mentors, teachers of my academic career and colleagues at Amity University Kolkata, who have fostered an environment of academic excellence and encouraged my research.

The countless mountaineers, trekkers, and expedition teams who have shared their experiences and allowed me to refine my understanding of high-altitude nutrition.

My team at RB Diet Clinic, unit of Clinical Nutrition and Wellness Solutions, whose dedication to our clients' health and well-being constantly inspires me to push the boundaries of nutritional science.

My publishers and editorial team, for their patience, insights, and commitment to bringing this book to life.

And finally, to all the high-altitude adventurers out there - your courage and determination to push the limits of human endurance have been the driving force behind this work.

Thank you all for being part of this journey to the heights of nutritional science.

Prologue

At 5,364 meters (17,598 feet) above sea level, the air is thin, and every breath is a conscious effort. While climbers prepare for their ascent to the roof of the world their faces are a mix of determination and apprehension. As a nutritionist, I know that their success doesn't just depend on their physical training or mental fortitude—it hinges significantly on what they put into their bodies.

High-altitude environments push human physiology to its limits. The reduced oxygen, extreme cold, and physical exertion create a perfect storm of metabolic challenges. In these conditions, proper nutrition isn't just about fueling the body; it's about survival.

Research has shown that how the right nutritional strategies can make the difference while travelling or climbing to high altitude places and a life-threatening situation. Research have also shown how inadequate nutrition can exacerbate altitude sickness, impair cognitive function, and lead to dangerous muscle loss.

This book is born from years of research, field experience, and a passion for helping adventurers reach new heights—literally. Whether you're planning to scale Everest, trek in the Andes, travel to Ladakh, Sela, Gurudongmar or embark on any high-altitude adventure, the knowledge within these pages will be your ally.

As we delve into the science of high-altitude nutrition, explore practical meal plans, and uncover the secrets of maintaining peak performance in thin air, remember: at high altitudes, every bite counts. Let this guide be your companion as you fuel your ascent, nourish your adventure, and elevate your experience.

Welcome to the world of high-altitude nutrition. Your journey to the top begins here.

ONE

THE HIGH-ALTITUDE CHALLENGE

The high-altitude challenge refers to the physical and physiological difficulties humans face when ascending to elevations significantly above sea level, typically above 2,400 meters (8,000 feet). At these heights, the air pressure is lower, which means there's less oxygen available in each breath. This presents a significant challenge for the human body, which is accustomed to operating at lower elevations.

Key challenges include:

Hypoxia:

Hypoxia is a condition where the body doesn't receive enough oxygen. At high altitudes, the lower air pressure means there's less oxygen available in each breath. This can lead to:

- Shortness of breath, especially during physical exertion
- Rapid heart rate as the body tries to circulate more oxygen
- Fatigue and weakness
- Impaired cognitive function, including poor decision-making and decreased alertness
- In severe cases, it can lead to High Altitude Pulmonary Edema (HAPE), a potentially life-threatening condition where fluid accumulates in the lungs

Altitude Sickness (Acute Mountain Sickness - AMS):

AMS typically occurs above 2,400 meters (8,000 feet) and can affect anyone, regardless of age or fitness level. Symptoms usually appear within 6-24 hours of ascent and include headache (the most common symptom), nausea and sometimes vomiting, dizziness and lightheadedness, loss of appetite, sleep disturbances, including insomnia, fatigue and weakness. In severe cases, it can progress to High Altitude Cerebral Edema (HACE), a life-threatening condition involving swelling of the brain

Increased Physical Exertion:

The lower oxygen levels mean that the body has to work harder to perform even simple tasks. This results in quicker fatigue during physical activities, longer recovery times after exertion, potential for overexertion, which can exacerbate other altitude-related issues and decreased overall performance in athletic activities.

Dehydration:

High altitude environments are often arid, and the body loses more water through increased respiration and perspiration. This leads to increased risk of dehydration, thickening of blood, which can increase the risk of clots, exacerbation of altitude sickness symptoms, and decreased urine output, which can be mistaken for proper hydration.

Temperature Extremes:

High altitude areas often experience more extreme and rapidly changing weather conditions. Cold temperatures can lead to hypothermia if not properly prepared, intense sunlight can cause severe sunburn and snow blindness, rapid weather changes can catch unprepared individuals off guard, wind chill can significantly lower the effective temperature.

UV Radiation:

The thinner atmosphere at high altitudes filters less UV radiation which increases risk of severe sunburn, even on cloudy days, higher risk of snow blindness in snowy environments, long-term increased risk of skin damage and potential skin cancers and potential damage to eyes without proper protection.

Sleep Disturbances:

At high altitude many people experience difficulty sleeping due to periodic breathing (alternating rapid breathing and apnea), general discomfort from other altitude-related symptoms and colder nighttime temperatures.

Decreased Appetite:

Many individuals experience a suppressed appetite at high altitudes, which can lead to insufficient calorie intake for the increased energy demands, potential nutritional deficiencies if prolonged and slower recovery and acclimatization.

Adequate Oxygenation:
Certain nutrients, like iron and vitamin B12, are essential for the production of red blood cells and optimal oxygen transport. Ensuring these nutrients are part of the diet can help maintain proper oxygenation of tissues.

Iron and Red Blood Cell Production:
High altitudes can lead to decreased oxygen levels in the blood, which can result in lower oxygen delivery to tissues. Iron is crucial for the production of red blood cells and hemoglobin, which transport oxygen. Ensuring an adequate intake of iron through diet or supplementation can be important at high altitudes.

Understanding these challenges is crucial for anyone planning high-altitude activities. Proper preparation, gradual ascent, and knowing how to recognize and respond to these issues can significantly reduce risks and improve the high-altitude experience.

ᖚᖚᖚ

Understanding High Altitude

Let's delve deeper into understanding high altitude. High altitude environments are typically categorized as follows:

- High altitude: 1,500-3,500 meters (5,000-11,500 feet)
- Very high altitude: 3,500-5,500 meters (11,500-18,000 feet)
- Extreme altitude: above 5,500 meters (18,000 feet)

There are several hidden challenges that are observed at high altitude and which affects our health adversely. As we ascend to higher altitudes, the atmosphere undergoes dramatic changes that significantly impact human physiology and survival. The most crucial change is the decrease in air pressure, which drops from 760 mmHg at sea level to a mere 380 mmHg at 5,500 meters. This reduction means fewer air molecules per breath, making oxygen acquisition challenging for the body.

While oxygen still constitutes 21% of the air, its partial pressure decreases, hindering its diffusion into the bloodstream. Temperature also plummets, dropping approximately 6.5°C per 1,000 meters of elevation gain. Conversely, UV radiation intensifies, increasing by 10-12% for every 1,000 meters climbed.

These atmospheric changes trigger various physiological responses. The body compensates through increased breathing rate, elevated heart rate, and heightened red blood cell production. Acclimatization, the process of adjusting to these conditions, typically begins within 1-3 days but may take weeks for complete adaptation.

Understanding these atmospheric changes is crucial for high-altitude travelers. It aids in recognizing potential health risks like Acute Mountain Sickness (AMS) and informs proper preparation. By respecting the body's need for gradual ascent and acclimatization, adventurers can ensure a safer and more enjoyable high-altitude experience.

High Altitude

ᐅᐅᐅ

The Importance of Nutrition

Now let us fuel your high-altitude adventure.

When venturing into high-altitude environments, proper nutrition becomes a cornerstone of health, performance, and safety. The human body faces unique challenges in these oxygen-scarce conditions, burning more calories even at rest. For every 1,000 meters above 5,000 feet, caloric needs can increase by 200-300 calories per day, necessitating a carefully planned diet.

Hydration is paramount in the dry, high-altitude air. Increased respiration and the arid environment accelerate fluid loss, making it crucial to consume at least 3-4 liters of water daily. Electrolyte-enhanced beverages can help maintain proper mineral balance, counteracting the effects of increased fluid loss.

Carbohydrates should take center stage in your high-altitude diet, comprising 60-70% of total caloric intake. This macronutrient helps maintain energy levels and may reduce the risk of altitude sickness. Additionally, adequate iron intake is vital to support the body's increased production of red blood cells, a natural response to the oxygen-poor environment.

Antioxidant-rich foods play a crucial role in combating the increased free radical production caused by heightened UV exposure and physical stress at high altitudes. Including a variety of colorful fruits and vegetables in your diet can provide these protective compounds. People with compromised absorption due to impaired gastrointestinal function, gut issues or gut dysbiosis or who consumes acid inhibitor drugs for a prolonged period of time, or levothyroxine for hypothyroidism can include 1 tablet multi vitamin and multi mineral daily in to their diet. Also before going for such high altitudes people should check their Vitamin D level to ensure adequacy. Previous studies found that vitamin D deficiency may induce acute respiratory distress syndrome (Grant et al., 2020), although local populations living in the high-altitude regions had less levels of vitamin D than those living at lower altitudes (Hirschler et al., 2019), along with low accidence of emphysema (Mendes et al., 2019) and are adapted to it. But people travelling from outside shall ensure Vit D3 corrected status to avoid respiratory distress at such high altitudes.

Research involving human subjects has highlighted the beneficial impact of antioxidant vitamins, particularly vitamins C and E, during the early phases of altitude adaptation. These vitamins were found to help combat oxidative stress and protect cell membrane integrity. Given that harsh weather conditions at high altitudes often restrict access to fresh produce, vitamin C supplementation is advised to maintain antioxidant levels in the body.

While nutrition is key, it's equally important to avoid certain substances. Alcohol and caffeine can exacerbate dehydration and potentially worsen altitude sickness symptoms, making them best avoided or consumed in strict moderation.

By prioritizing proper nutrition, high-altitude adventurers can maintain energy levels, support overall health, aid acclimatization, and reduce the risk of altitude-related illnesses. A well-planned nutritional strategy is not just beneficial—it's an essential component of any successful high-altitude expedition or activity, helping to ensure a safer and more enjoyable experience in these challenging environments.

ϷϷϷ

Preparing for Altitude: A Crucial Step for High-Elevation Adventures

Venturing into high-altitude environments requires careful preparation to ensure safety and enjoyment. The key to a successful ascent lies in understanding and respecting the body's need for acclimatization.

Preparing for High Altitude

Gradual ascent is paramount. The general rule is to increase sleeping altitude by no more than 300-500 meters per day once above 3,000 meters. This allows the body to adapt to the decreasing oxygen levels, reducing the risk of altitude sickness.

Physical fitness plays a crucial role. While it doesn't prevent altitude sickness, being in good shape can make the ascent less strenuous. Incorporate cardiovascular exercises and strength training in the pre-trip routine.

Hydration is critical at high altitudes. Begin hydrating well before the trip and maintain fluid intake throughout. To aim for clear or light-colored urine as an indicator of good hydration.

Medication like acetazolamide (Diamox) for preventing altitude sickness can be considered by consulting a clinician. Some find that ginger or coca tea helps with symptoms.

Mental preparation is equally important. One need to understand the symptoms of altitude sickness and to be prepared to descend if necessary. It is to be remembered that no view is worth risking the health.

By preparing thoroughly, one set the stage for a safer and more enjoyable high-altitude experience.

TWO

HEALTH AND SAFETY AT ALTITUDE: UNDERSTANDING AND MANAGING ALTITUDE-RELATED CHALLENGES

As more people venture into high-altitude environments for work, sport, or leisure, understanding the health implications of altitude exposure becomes crucial. Here two critical aspects of altitude health: altitude sickness and the management of pre-existing medical conditions at high elevations has been explored.

Altitude Sickness

Altitude sickness, also known as *Acute Mountain Sickness (AMS)*, is a collection of symptoms that can occur when ascending to high altitudes too quickly. It typically affects individuals at elevations above 2,500 meters (8,200 feet), though susceptibility varies among individuals.

Recognizing Symptoms:

1. Mild AMS:

· Headache

- Fatigue
- Dizziness
- Loss of appetite
- Nausea
- Difficulty sleeping

2. Moderate to Severe AMS:

- Severe headache resistant to medication
- Persistent vomiting
- Shortness of breath at rest
- Decreased coordination (ataxia)
- Confusion
- Fluid buildup in the lungs (High Altitude Pulmonary Edema - HAPE)
- Fluid buildup in the brain (High Altitude Cerebral Edema - HACE)

It's crucial to recognize these symptoms early, as severe forms of altitude sickness can be life-threatening if not addressed promptly.

Altitude and Medical Conditions

Individuals with pre-existing medical conditions face additional challenges at high altitudes. Understanding these challenges and implementing proper management strategies is crucial for safe altitude experiences.

Managing Chronic Health Issues:

1. Cardiovascular Conditions:

- The heart works harder at altitude due to lower oxygen levels.
- Individuals with heart conditions should consult their physician before traveling to high altitudes.
- Gradual ascent and proper acclimatization are crucial.
- Monitor blood pressure and heart rate regularly.
- Be aware of increased risk of arrhythmias and adjust medications if necessary under medical supervision.

2. Respiratory Conditions (e.g., Asthma, COPD):

- Cold, dry air at altitude can exacerbate respiratory conditions.
- Carry all necessary medications, including rescue inhalers.

- Use a face mask or scarf to warm and humidify inhaled air.
- Consider using supplemental oxygen, especially during sleep.

3. Diabetes:

- Altitude can affect blood glucose levels and insulin requirements.
- Monitor blood sugar more frequently than usual.
- Be aware that glucometers may be less accurate at high altitudes.
- Protect insulin and other medications from extreme temperatures.

4. Anemia:

- Anemic individuals may struggle more with the reduced oxygen at altitude.
- Consult with a physician about iron supplementation before travel.
- Consider a pre-travel hemoglobin check and possible treatment.

5. Pregnancy:

- Pregnant women should avoid high altitudes, especially in the third trimester.
- If travel is necessary, careful monitoring and gradual ascent are crucial.

6. Sleep Apnea:

- Sleep apnea can worsen at altitude, increasing the risk of altitude sickness.
- Bring CPAP equipment if used, and consider using supplemental oxygen.

7. Hypertension:

- Blood pressure may increase at altitude.
- Monitor blood pressure regularly and adjust medications as needed under physician guidance.

General Management Strategies:
1. ***Pre-Travel Preparation:*** Consult with healthcare providers well in advance of travel. Obtain sufficient medication supplies, including extras

for potential delays. Carry a detailed medical history and medication list.

2. **_Gradual Ascent:_** Allow time for acclimatization, ascending no more than 300-500 meters per day above 3,000 meters. Include rest days in your itinerary.

3. **_Stay Informed:_** Research medical facilities available at your destination. Consider travel insurance that covers high-altitude evacuation.

4. **_Listen to Your Body:_** Be aware of any changes in your condition. Don't hesitate to descend if symptoms worsen.

5. **_Supplemental Oxygen:_** Consider using supplemental oxygen, especially for sleep, if you have a chronic condition that affects oxygenation.

Understanding and preparing for the challenges of high-altitude environments is crucial for both the prevention and management of altitude-related health issues. By recognizing the symptoms of altitude sickness, implementing appropriate nutritional strategies, and carefully managing pre-existing medical conditions, individuals can significantly reduce their risk of altitude-related complications. Remember, when it comes to altitude health, prevention, preparation, and prompt response to symptoms are key to ensuring a safe and enjoyable high-altitude experience.

THREE
PRE-EXPEDITION NUTRITION PLANNING

Pre-Expedition Nutrition Planning: Fueling Success at High Altitudes

Proper nutrition is a cornerstone of any successful high-altitude expedition. Careful planning and preparation can significantly impact performance, health, and overall expedition success. Here we explored two crucial aspects of pre-expedition nutrition planning: assessing individual needs and creating a nutritional strategy.

Preparing for espedition

Assessing Individual Needs Creating a Nutritional Strategy

Before embarking on a high-altitude journey, it's essential to evaluate each team member's unique nutritional requirements. Tailoring nutrition is the key to high-altitude success.

When planning for high-altitude expeditions, one size doesn't fit all. Assessing individual nutritional needs is crucial for team success and safety. This process begins with evaluating each member's baseline health and fitness, considering existing conditions and overall physical preparedness. Body composition plays a significant role, as weight, muscle mass, and body fat percentage influence caloric and nutrient requirements.

Age and gender are essential factors, affecting metabolism and nutritional needs. The expedition role – whether climber, support staff, or guide – dictates energy demands and nutritional strategy. Personal dietary preferences and restrictions, including vegetarian, vegan, or allergy-related needs, must be accommodated without compromising nutritional adequacy.

Previous high-altitude experiences offer valuable insights into individual responses to altitude and specific nutritional needs. Understanding each person's metabolic rate is crucial, as some naturally burn more calories than others.

Additional considerations include medication interactions, stress response, sleep patterns, and potential taste sensitivity changes at altitude. By meticulously assessing these individual factors, expedition planners can craft personalized nutrition strategies that optimize performance, health, and enjoyment for each team member. This tailored approach significantly enhances the likelihood of a successful and safe high-altitude adventure.

ᐳᐳᐳ

Creating a Nutritional Strategy: Fueling Success at High Altitudes

Developing a comprehensive nutritional strategy is crucial for the success and safety of high-altitude expeditions. This process involves careful planning and consideration of the unique challenges posed by elevated environments.

A well-crafted nutritional strategy addresses the increased caloric demands at high altitudes, where the body burns more energy even at rest. It also accounts for the need for proper hydration in the often dry, thin air. The strategy should balance macronutrients, with a focus on easily digestible carbohydrates for quick energy.

Importantly, a good nutritional plan goes beyond just calories and hydration. It considers the role of specific nutrients like iron for increased red blood cell production and antioxidants to combat the effects of increased UV exposure. The strategy should also account for practical aspects such as food weight, ease of preparation, and palatability at altitude.

By creating a tailored nutritional strategy, expedition teams can optimize their dietary approach to meet the unique demands of high-altitude environments, supporting physical performance, aiding acclimatization, and reducing the risk of altitude-related illnesses.

FOUR

HYDRATION AT HIGH ALTITUDE: A CRITICAL COMPONENT OF MOUNTAIN SAFETY

Proper hydration is paramount when venturing into high-altitude environments. The combination of decreased humidity, increased respiratory rate, and elevated physical exertion leads to accelerated fluid loss, making dehydration a significant risk for mountaineers and high-altitude trekkers.

At high altitudes, the body's thirst response can be dulled, masking the need for fluids. Simultaneously, increased urination—a common effect of altitude—can further contribute to dehydration. These factors necessitate a proactive approach to hydration.

Experts recommend consuming 3-4 liters of water daily at high altitudes. However, individual needs may vary based on factors such as activity level, temperature, and personal physiology. Monitoring urine color—aiming for pale yellow—can serve as a practical indicator of hydration status.

While water is essential, electrolyte balance is equally crucial. The increased respiration and perspiration at altitude can deplete the body's electrolyte stores. Incorporating electrolyte-rich beverages or supplements can help maintain this delicate balance.

It's important to note that overhydration, or hyponatremia, can also pose risks. Balance is key. By prioritizing consistent, appropriate fluid intake, high-altitude adventurers can significantly enhance their safety, performance, and overall experience in these challenging environments.

Dehydration Risks: A Silent Threat at High Altitudes

In high-altitude settings, dehydration poses a significant and often underestimated risk to climbers and trekkers. The combination of low humidity, increased respiratory rate, and intensified physical exertion creates a perfect storm for rapid fluid loss, far exceeding what many experience at lower elevations.

The dangers of dehydration at altitude are multifaceted. Reduced blood volume can impair the body's ability to acclimatize, potentially exacerbating symptoms of altitude sickness. Cognitive function may decline, leading to poor decision-making—a critical risk in challenging mountain environments. Physical performance suffers as well, with dehydration causing fatigue, reduced endurance, and increased susceptibility to cold injuries.

Moreover, dehydration can mask or mimic symptoms of altitude illness, complicating diagnosis and appropriate treatment. Headaches, fatigue, and dizziness—common to both dehydration and Acute Mountain Sickness—can lead to confusion about the underlying cause.

The body's thirst mechanism often becomes less reliable at altitude, failing to signal the need for fluids accurately. This physiological quirk, combined with the cold-induced suppression of thirst, means that conscious, deliberate hydration is essential.

Recognizing these risks, mountaineers or travellers of high altitude must prioritize regular fluid intake, regardless of thirst sensation. Monitoring urine output and color provides a practical method for assessing hydration status in the field. By staying vigilant about hydration, high-altitude adventurers can significantly mitigate one of the most pervasive risks in mountain environments.

Optimal Hydration Strategies: Mastering Fluid Balance at High Altitudes

Maintaining proper hydration at high altitudes requires a strategic approach that goes beyond simply drinking water. Effective hydration strategies are crucial for performance, safety, and acclimatization in these challenging environments.

First and foremost, begin hydrating well before ascent. Arrive at altitude in a well-hydrated state to give your body a head start. Aim to consume 3-4 liters of fluid daily, adjusting based on activity level and personal needs.

Sip regularly throughout the day rather than gulping large amounts infrequently.

Incorporate electrolyte-rich beverages to maintain mineral balance. Sports drinks, electrolyte tablets, or even homemade solutions can help replace salts lost through increased respiration and perspiration. However, be cautious with caffeine and alcohol, as these can contribute to dehydration.

Monitor your hydration status by checking urine color (aim for pale yellow) and output frequency. In cold environments, use insulated containers to prevent water from freezing and to encourage more frequent drinking.

Consider warm beverages, which can be more appealing in cold conditions and provide additional comfort. Soups and broths offer both hydration and valuable nutrients.

Remember, thirst is not a reliable indicator at altitude. Develop a consistent drinking schedule and stick to it, even when not feeling thirsty. By implementing these strategies, high-altitude adventurers can optimize their hydration, enhancing both safety and performance in the mountains.

FIVE

HIGH-ALTITUDE NUTRITION BASICS: FUELING YOUR BODY IN THIN AIR

Venturing into high-altitude environments presents unique challenges to the human body, and proper nutrition plays a crucial role in meeting these challenges head-on. As we ascend to elevations above 2,400 meters (8,000 feet), our bodies face increased metabolic demands, altered digestion, and a heightened risk of dehydration.

This guide explores the essential aspects of high-altitude nutrition, from understanding the body's changing needs to implementing effective strategies for maintaining health and performance in oxygen-scarce environments. Whether you're a mountaineer tackling extreme altitudes, a trekker exploring high passes, or simply visiting a high-elevation destination, the principles outlined here will help you optimize your nutritional approach.

We'll delve into topics such as increased caloric requirements, the importance of proper hydration, macronutrient balance, and the role of specific nutrients in altitude adaptation. By understanding and applying these high-altitude nutrition basics, you'll be better equipped to enjoy your mountain adventures safely and effectively.

Remember, proper nutrition at high altitudes is not just about fueling your body—it's a critical component of acclimatization, performance, and overall well-being in these challenging environments.

Macronutrients at Altitude

When ascending to high altitudes, the body's nutritional needs undergo significant changes. Understanding how to balance macronutrients—carbohydrates, proteins, and fats—becomes crucial for maintaining energy, supporting acclimatization, and ensuring overall well-being in oxygen-scarce environments.

At high altitudes, the body's metabolism shifts, often favoring carbohydrates as the primary fuel source. This adjustment, coupled with increased energy expenditure even at rest, necessitates a recalibration of macronutrient intake. The traditional balance of macronutrients often needs modification to meet the unique demands of high-altitude physiology.

Carbohydrates take on heightened importance, providing readily available energy and potentially aiding in the prevention of altitude sickness. Protein requirements may change to support increased red blood cell production and tissue repair. Fats, while still essential, may need to be consumed judiciously due to potential digestive challenges at altitude.

In this guide, we'll explore the optimal ratios of macronutrients for high-altitude adventures, discuss how each macronutrient contributes to performance and adaptation, and provide practical tips for incorporating these principles into your high-altitude diet. By mastering the balance of macronutrients, you'll be better equipped to fuel your body effectively, enhance your performance, and enjoy a safer, more comfortable experience in the mountains.

ᑭᑭᑭ

Carbohydrates: The Energy Source

At high altitudes, carbohydrates become the body's preferred fuel, playing a crucial role in maintaining energy levels and supporting acclimatization. The reduced oxygen availability at elevation makes carbohydrates an efficient energy source, as they require less oxygen for metabolism compared to fats.

It is recommended that carbohydrates should comprise 60-70% of total caloric intake at high altitudes. This increased proportion helps maintain blood glucose levels, providing readily available energy for both physical exertion and basic bodily functions.

Complex carbohydrates, such as whole grains, legumes, and starchy vegetables, offer sustained energy release. These should form the foundation of the diet. Simple carbohydrates, like fruits and sports gels, provide quick energy boosts useful during intense activities.

Carbohydrate intake may also help mitigate the risk of acute mountain sickness. Some studies suggest that a high-carbohydrate diet can improve oxygen saturation in the blood, potentially easing altitude adaptation.

However, it's important to choose easily digestible carbohydrates, as the digestive system can be more sensitive at altitude. Oatmeal, rice, pasta, and potatoes are excellent options.

By prioritizing carbohydrates in your high-altitude diet, you provide your body with the optimal fuel to meet the increased energy demands and unique challenges of mountain environments.

ᐳᐳᐳ

Protein: Muscle Maintenance at High Altitudes

While carbohydrates take center stage in high-altitude nutrition, protein plays a crucial supporting role, particularly in maintaining muscle mass and supporting the body's adaptation to altitude.

At high elevations, the body experiences increased protein breakdown, partly due to the stress of altitude and increased physical exertion. To counteract this, a moderate increase in protein intake is recommended. Aiming for about 1.2 to 1.4 grams of protein per kilogram of body weight daily, compared to the 0.8 grams typically is recommended at such sea level.

Protein is essential for repairing and rebuilding muscle tissue, which is particularly important given the increased physical demands of high-altitude activities. It also supports the production of red blood cells, a key aspect of altitude acclimatization.

However, it's important not to overemphasize protein consumption. Excessive protein intake can be hard on the kidneys and may contribute to dehydration, already a risk at altitude.

Good protein sources for high-altitude expeditions include lean meats, fish, eggs, dairy products, and plant-based options like legumes and nuts. Portable protein sources such as jerky or protein bars can be valuable for on-the-go nutrition.

By maintaining adequate protein intake, one can support their body's repair processes and adaptation mechanisms, contributing to better performance and recovery in high-altitude environments.

ᐳᐳᐳ

Fat: Energy Reserves for High-Altitude Endurance

While carbohydrates are the primary fuel source at high altitudes, fats play a crucial role in providing sustained energy and supporting overall health in these challenging environments.

At high elevations, fat should comprise about 20-25% of total caloric intake. This is slightly lower than recommendations for sea level, reflecting the body's preference for carbohydrates in oxygen-scarce conditions. However, fats remain essential for several reasons.

Fats are the most calorie-dense macronutrient, providing 9 calories per gram compared to 4 for carbohydrates and proteins. This makes them valuable for meeting increased caloric needs without excessive food volume, which can be challenging at altitude where appetite is often suppressed.

Moreover, fats are crucial for maintaining body temperature in cold mountain environments. They also play a vital role in hormone production and the absorption of fat-soluble vitamins (A, D, E, and K), which are important for overall health and altitude adaptation.

Good sources of fats for high-altitude expeditions include nuts, seeds, avocados, olive oil, and fatty fish. These provide a mix of saturated and unsaturated fats, including omega-3 fatty acids beneficial for reducing inflammation.

While fat intake should be moderated at high altitudes, including adequate healthy fats in your diet supports energy reserves, hormonal balance, and overall nutritional status, contributing to better endurance and performance in mountain environments.

SIX

MICRONUTRIENTS AND ALTITUDE: THE HIDDEN HEROES OF HIGH-ELEVATION NUTRITION

While macronutrients often take center stage in discussions of high-altitude nutrition, micronutrients play an equally crucial role in supporting the body's adaptation to oxygen-scarce environments. These vitamins and minerals, though required in smaller quantities, are essential for maintaining health, enhancing performance, and facilitating acclimatization at high elevations.

At altitude, the body undergoes significant physiological changes that can alter micronutrient needs and utilization. Increased oxidative stress, accelerated red blood cell production, and changes in fluid balance all impact the body's micronutrient requirements. Understanding these shifts is key to optimizing nutrition for high-altitude adventures.

This section explores the roles of various micronutrients in high-altitude physiology. We'll delve into the importance of iron for boosting oxygen-carrying capacity, the role of antioxidants like vitamins C and E in combating altitude-induced oxidative stress, and the significance of electrolytes in maintaining hydration and muscle function.

We'll also discuss how altitude can affect the absorption and metabolism of certain micronutrients, and provide strategies for ensuring adequate intake in challenging mountain environments. From the B-vitamins crucial for energy metabolism to minerals like zinc and selenium that support immune function, we'll cover the full spectrum of micronutrients relevant to high-altitude performance.

By understanding the vital roles of these "hidden heroes," you'll be better equipped to fine-tune your nutritional approach, supporting your body's complex adaptation processes and enhancing your overall experience in the high mountains. Let's explore how these tiny but mighty nutrients can make a big difference in your high-altitude adventures.

ᑭᑭᑭ

Vitamins and Minerals

Proper nutrition, with a focus on essential vitamins and minerals, plays a crucial role in maintaining health and performance at high altitudes. By understanding the unique nutritional demands of these environments and implementing targeted strategies, adventurers can optimize their physiological adaptation and enhance their overall high-altitude experience. As research in this field continues to evolve, staying informed about the latest nutritional recommendations for high-altitude health remains an important aspect of responsible mountaineering and alpine exploration.

Below points are to be considered while planning the meals to meet up the micronutrient requirements.

Increased Needs:

Iron: At high altitudes, the body produces more red blood cells to compensate for lower oxygen levels. This process, called erythropoiesis, requires increased iron. Iron-rich foods like red meat, legumes, and leafy greens become crucial. Some climbers or high-altitude residents may benefit from iron supplements, but this should be done under medical supervision to avoid iron overload.

Antioxidants: The body experiences increased oxidative stress at high altitudes due to lower oxygen levels and increased UV radiation exposure. Vitamins C and E, along with beta-carotene, help combat this stress. Foods rich in these nutrients include citrus fruits, berries, nuts, seeds, and colorful vegetables.

B Vitamins: The body's energy metabolism increases at high altitudes to cope with the challenging environment. B vitamins, particularly B1 (thiamine), B2 (riboflavin), and B3 (niacin), are essential for energy production. Good sources include whole grains, lean meats, eggs, and fortified cereals.

Specific Considerations:

Vitamin D: In some high-altitude environments, especially during winter months or in areas with limited sunlight, vitamin D deficiency can be a concern. The body produces vitamin D when skin is exposed to sunlight. In these conditions, dietary sources (fatty fish, egg yolks, fortified foods) or supplements may be necessary.

Electrolytes: High altitudes often lead to increased fluid loss through respiration and sweating. This can deplete electrolytes like sodium, potassium, and magnesium. Balanced electrolyte intake is crucial for proper hydration and muscle function. Sports drinks, bananas, nuts, and leafy greens can help replenish these minerals.

Challenges:

Reduced Appetite: Many people experience a decrease in appetite at high altitudes, which can lead to inadequate calorie and nutrient intake. This makes it even more important to focus on nutrient-dense foods and possibly use meal replacement shakes or bars fortified with vitamins and minerals.

- Strategies to address reduced appetite:
- Focus on nutrient-dense, calorie-rich foods
- Eat smaller, more frequent meals
- Consider liquid calories (e.g., smoothies, meal replacement shakes)

ᚦᚦᚦ

Dehydration: The dry air and increased respiration rate at high altitudes can lead to faster dehydration. This not only affects overall health but can also impair nutrient absorption in the gut. Staying well-hydrated is crucial for maintaining proper nutrient balance.

Changes in water metabolism during altitude exposure can interfere with measurements of energy balance and body weight changes. During acclimatization, a decrease in intra- and extra-cellular water occurs, as well as a decrease in circulating plasma volume. These changes result in a weight loss of 1-2 kg . By contrast, a temporary increase of body water may be observed during the initial stage at altitude if there are symptoms of acute mountain sick- ness. It has been estimated that during climbing water loss would be very high due to the inhalation of dry air and to hy- perventilation, increasing water intake levels.

Cold-induced diuresis at HA, hyperventilation along with the dry environment at altitude makes individuals prone to hypohydration. Acute exposure to moderate altitude causes transient hypohydration which is due to increased diuresis and an acute reduction in fluid intake due to a decrease in thirst.

Hydration tips at High Altitude

Pre-Hydrate

The best way to beat high altitude dehydration is to stay ahead of it. Drink plenty of water in the days and hours before heading to a high altitude destination. Whether you're sitting in the car, airplane, or on your way to the trailhead, drinking water should be a part of your preparation for excursions at elevation.

Start Slow

Ease into your activity. Especially if you're not used to high altitude, your body will have to work harder in these conditions. If possible, give your body time to acclimate and rest before jumping into a race or intense exercise. This can also mean ascending gradually versus going from zero to 10,000 feet in a single day.

Consume Hydrating Foods

Besides drinking water, you can support hydration by eating foods with a high water content like apples, cucumbers, melons, strawberries, broccoli, celery, zucchini, and lettuce. These foods won't replace your necessary water intake—rather they supplement it.

Moderate Caffeine and Alcohol

Alcohol and caffeine are diuretics, which means they promote increased urine production. Given that you'll already be going for more "bio breaks" at high altitude, you don't want to exacerbate that. Try to focus on water and other hydrating beverages, consume in moderation, or save your cocktail or craft beer for an apres-ski reward.

Drink Consistently Throughout the Day

Make drinking water at high altitude an ongoing thing. Plan for hydration breaks throughout the day and bring a reusable water bottle or hydration bladder with you so that water is always within reach. CamelBak has a full line of hydration packs for snow and winter sports, designed to prevent your water from freezing and keep you sipping throughout the day.

Balance with Electrolytes

People often wonder about Pedialyte, sports drinks, electrolyte drinks or electrolyte powder mixes for staying hydrated in high altitude. Electrolyte balance is critical for peak performance and avoiding dehydration. This is especially true in high altitudes, as you need to replace the salt your body is losing via sweat and increased respiration and urination.

ᗡᗡᗡ

Additional Recommendations:

*Zinc:*This mineral supports immune function, which can be compromised at high altitudes. Good sources include oysters, beef, pumpkin seeds, and lentils.

Omega-3 Fatty Acids: These may help with altitude adaptation and reducing inflammation. Sources include fatty fish, flaxseeds, and walnuts.

Calcium: Important for bone health, especially during extended high-altitude stays. Dairy products, fortified plant milks, and leafy greens are good sources.

Practical Tips:

- Plan meals and snacks in advance, focusing on nutrient-dense, easily digestible foods.
- Consider using a multivitamin supplement designed for high-altitude conditions.
- Drink plenty of water and electrolyte-rich beverages throughout the day.
- Monitor urine color as an indicator of hydration status (pale yellow is ideal).
- Be aware of potential interactions between supplements and medications, especially those used for altitude sickness.

Remember, individual needs can vary based on factors like altitude, duration of stay, physical activity level, and personal health conditions. Consulting with a nutritionist or doctor experienced in high-altitude health can provide personalized recommendations.

ᗡᗡᗡ

The Crucial Role of Antioxidants at High Altitudes: Combating Oxidative Stress in Thin Air

As adventurers and mountaineers ascend to breathtaking heights, their bodies face a myriad of challenges. Among these, the increased oxidative stress at high altitudes stands out as a significant concern. This article delves into the vital role of antioxidants in protecting the human body against the heightened oxidative damage experienced in high-altitude environments.

Understanding Oxidative Stress at High Altitudes:

At elevations above 2,500 meters (8,200 feet), the human body encounters a perfect storm of factors that contribute to increased oxidative stress. The primary culprits include:

1. Hypoxia: The reduced oxygen availability at high altitudes leads to a paradoxical increase in the production of reactive oxygen species (ROS) within cells. This occurs as the mitochondria, our cellular powerhouses, struggle to maintain energy production with limited oxygen.

2. Increased UV Radiation: As altitude increases, the atmosphere thins, allowing more ultraviolet (UV) radiation to penetrate. This heightened UV exposure can directly damage cellular components and trigger the formation of free radicals.

3. Physical Exertion: The demanding nature of high-altitude activities, such as climbing or trekking, increases metabolic rate and oxygen consumption. This, in turn, leads to greater production of ROS as a byproduct of energy metabolism.

4. Cold Temperatures: Many high-altitude environments are characterized by low temperatures, which can induce the production of stress hormones and, consequently, increase oxidative stress.

The Antioxidant Arsenal:

To combat the onslaught of free radicals and oxidative damage, the body relies on a sophisticated network of antioxidants. Key players in this defensive lineup include:

1. Vitamin C (Ascorbic Acid):

- Function: A powerful water-soluble antioxidant that neutralizes a wide range of free radicals.
- High-Altitude Benefit: Helps regenerate other antioxidants and supports the immune system, which can be compromised at altitude.
- Food Sources: Citrus fruits, berries, kiwi, bell peppers, and broccoli.

2. Vitamin E (Tocopherols):

- Function: A fat-soluble antioxidant that protects cell membranes from lipid peroxidation.
- High-Altitude Benefit: Shields red blood cells from oxidative damage, crucial for maintaining oxygen-carrying capacity.
- Food Sources: Nuts, seeds, avocados, and vegetable oils.

3. Beta-Carotene:

- Function: A precursor to vitamin A and a potent antioxidant in its own right.
- High-Altitude Benefit: Offers protection against UV-induced oxidative stress.
- Food Sources: Orange and yellow fruits and vegetables, leafy greens.

4. Selenium:

- Function: An essential component of several antioxidant enzymes, including glutathione peroxidase.
- High-Altitude Benefit: Supports overall antioxidant function and may help in altitude acclimatization.
- Food Sources: Brazil nuts, seafood, poultry, and whole grains.

5. Flavonoids:

- Function: A diverse group of plant-based compounds with potent antioxidant properties.
- High-Altitude Benefit: Offer broad-spectrum protection against various forms of oxidative stress.
- Food Sources: Berries, dark chocolate, green tea, and red wine.

Optimizing Antioxidant Intake at High Altitudes:
While the exact antioxidant requirements for high-altitude exposure remain a subject of ongoing research, several strategies can help optimize intake:

- Diverse, Colorful Diet: Emphasize a variety of fruits and vegetables, aiming for a rainbow of colors to ensure a broad spectrum of antioxidants.

- Pre-Altitude Loading: Consider increasing antioxidant-rich foods in the days leading up to high-altitude exposure to build up reserves.
- Portable Options: Pack antioxidant-rich snacks such as dried fruits, nuts, and dark chocolate for on-the-go consumption during high-altitude activities.
- Hydration with Benefits: Incorporate antioxidant-rich beverages like green tea or fruit-infused water to combine hydration with antioxidant intake.
- Supplementation Considerations: While whole food sources are preferred, supplementation may be beneficial in some cases. However, this should be approached cautiously and under medical guidance, as excessive antioxidant supplementation can potentially interfere with altitude acclimatization processes.

The importance of antioxidants in high-altitude environments cannot be overstated. As our bodies grapple with the increased oxidative stress induced by thin air, intense UV radiation, and physical exertion, a robust antioxidant defense becomes crucial. By understanding the unique challenges posed by high altitudes and strategically incorporating antioxidant-rich foods into their diets, mountaineers and high-altitude travelers can better protect their bodies against oxidative damage. This not only supports overall health but may also enhance performance and recovery in these demanding environments.

As research in this field continues to evolve, maintaining an awareness of the latest findings on antioxidant needs at high altitudes will be essential for anyone venturing into the world's loftiest regions. With the right nutritional strategies, including a focus on antioxidants, adventurers can better equip their bodies to thrive in the rarefied air of high-altitude landscapes.

ÞÞÞ

Electrolyte Balance at High Altitudes: The Key to Peak Performance and Health

As adventurers ascend to lofty heights, they face numerous physiological challenges. Among these, maintaining proper electrolyte balance becomes crucial for both performance and well-being. Here we explores the vital role of electrolytes at high altitudes, their importance, and strategies for maintaining optimal levels in these demanding environments.

Electrolytes are minerals in our blood and other bodily fluids that carry an electric charge. They play essential roles in hydration, nerve and muscle function, blood pH, tissue repair, and nutrient transportation. The primary electrolytes include:

Sodium

Potassium

Calcium

Magnesium

Chloride

Bicarbonate

The High-Altitude Challenge:

At elevations above 2,500 meters (8,200 feet), several factors contribute to electrolyte imbalance:

Increased Respiratory Rate: The body's natural response to lower oxygen levels is to breathe faster and more deeply. This hyperventilation leads to greater water loss through respiration.

Increased Urine Output: A phenomenon known as altitude diuresis occurs in the first few days at altitude, causing increased urine production and subsequent fluid and electrolyte loss.

Sweating: Physical exertion at altitude, often coupled with layered clothing, can lead to significant sweat loss, depleting both fluids and electrolytes.

Gastrointestinal Issues: Many people experience decreased appetite or gastrointestinal distress at altitude, potentially leading to reduced food and fluid intake.

Cold-Induced Diuresis: Exposure to cold temperatures, common at high altitudes, can increase urine output.

Importance of Electrolyte Balance at Altitude:

Maintaining proper electrolyte levels is critical for several reasons:

- *Hydration:* Electrolytes help regulate fluid balance between intracellular and extracellular compartments, crucial for proper hydration.
- *Muscle Function:* Electrolytes, particularly sodium and potassium, are essential for proper muscle contraction and relaxation.
- *Nerve Transmission:* Balanced electrolytes ensure proper nerve signaling, vital for coordination and cognitive function.
- *Altitude Acclimatization:* Proper electrolyte balance may aid in the body's adaptation to high-altitude environments.

- ***Prevention of Altitude Illness:*** While not a cure-all, maintaining electrolyte balance can help mitigate some symptoms associated with acute mountain sickness.

Key Electrolytes at High Altitude:

Sodium:

Function: Regulates fluid balance, aids nerve and muscle function.

High-Altitude Consideration: Lost through sweat and urine; crucial for maintaining blood volume.

Sources: Salt, sports drinks, crackers, pretzels.

Potassium:

Function: Supports heart function, muscle contraction, and nerve transmission.

High-Altitude Consideration: Helps counterbalance sodium and maintains proper cell function.

Sources: Bananas, potatoes, avocados, dried fruits.

Magnesium:

Function: Involved in over 300 enzymatic reactions, including energy production and muscle function.

High-Altitude Consideration: May help with sleep quality and muscle recovery at altitude.

Sources: Nuts, seeds, whole grains, leafy greens.

Calcium:

Function: Essential for bone health, muscle contraction, and nerve function.

High-Altitude Consideration: Supports muscle function during increased physical exertion.

Sources: Dairy products, fortified plant milks, leafy greens.

Strategies for Maintaining Electrolyte Balance:

- Hydration with Electrolytes:
- Consume electrolyte-rich beverages, not just plain water.
- Consider using sports drinks or electrolyte tablets in your water.

Balanced Diet:

- Emphasize whole foods rich in natural electrolytes.
- Include salty snacks to replace sodium lost through sweat.

Monitor Urine Color:

- Aim for pale yellow urine as an indicator of good hydration.

Gradual Ascent:

- Allow time for acclimatization to minimize altitude diuresis.

Appropriate Clothing:

- Dress in layers to prevent excessive sweating and subsequent electrolyte loss.

Supplementation:

- Consider electrolyte supplements, especially during prolonged activity post consultation with health care professional.

Mindful Alcohol Consumption:

- Limit alcohol intake, as it can exacerbate dehydration and electrolyte imbalance.

Maintaining electrolyte balance at high altitudes is a critical yet often overlooked aspect of mountain health and performance. The unique physiological stresses of high-altitude environments demand careful attention to hydration and mineral intake. By understanding the importance of electrolytes and implementing strategies to maintain their balance, adventurers can enhance their body's ability to adapt to altitude, improve performance, and reduce the risk of altitude-related illnesses.

As research in high-altitude physiology continues to advance, staying informed about best practices for electrolyte management will remain crucial for anyone venturing into the world's high places. With proper planning and awareness, maintaining electrolyte balance can become an integral part of a successful and healthy high-altitude experience.

SEVEN

Nutrition Strategies At Your Rescue

Nutritional Strategies to Combat Physiological and Biochemical Changes in Adult Males and Females at Higher Altitudes

Moving to higher altitudes can cause physiological and biochemical changes in adult males and females, leading to a range of symptoms, including skeletal muscle changes, cramps, and dizziness. Proper nutrition can help combat these changes and alleviate symptoms, allowing individuals to acclimate to the hypoxic environment more effectively. Changes in nutrient requirements as compared to Recommnded Dietary Allowances are as follows :

Macro-Nutrient Changes:

Macronutrients, such as carbohydrates, proteins, and fats, are critical for energy production and maintaining proper bodily function. In higher altitude environments, individuals may need to adjust their macronutrient intake to combat the changes in their bodies, including:

Increased Carbohydrate Intake: As the body requires more energy to acclimate to the hypoxic environment, individuals may need to increase their carbohydrate intake to meet their energy needs.

Adequate Protein Intake: Protein is essential for muscle repair and recovery. As skeletal muscle changes and cramps can occur at higher altitudes, individuals may need to ensure they are consuming adequate protein to maintain muscle mass.

Increased Fat Intake: Fat is a critical energy source, particularly during prolonged physical activity. Increasing fat intake can help provide energy during activities such as hiking and climbing.

Micro-Nutrient Changes:

Micronutrients, such as vitamins and minerals, are essential for a range of bodily functions, including energy production, immune function, and maintaining bone health. In higher altitude environments, individuals may need to adjust their micronutrient intake to combat the changes in their bodies, including:

Increased Iron Intake: Iron is essential for oxygen transport in the blood. As the body requires more oxygen at higher altitudes, individuals may need to increase their iron intake to ensure proper oxygen delivery to the tissues.

Adequate Vitamin C and E Intake: Vitamin C and E are antioxidants that protect against oxidative stress, which can increase at higher altitudes due to increased physical activity and hypoxic stress.

Increased Calcium and Vitamin D Intake: Calcium and vitamin D are critical for maintaining bone health. As bone resorption can increase at higher altitudes, individuals may need to increase their calcium and vitamin D intake to prevent bone loss.

Hydration:

Proper hydration is essential at higher altitudes to prevent dehydration and its associated complications, including headaches, dizziness, and fatigue. Individuals should aim to consume adequate fluids and electrolytes to maintain proper hydration levels.

Staying hydrated is important at high altitudes

Proper nutrition is critical for combating the physiological and biochemical changes that occur in adult males and females at higher altitudes. Adequate intake of macronutrients, micronutrients, and proper hydration can help alleviate symptoms and allow individuals to acclimate more effectively to the hypoxic environment.

Ways To Ensure Adequate Nutrition In High Altitude

- Begin your day with a wholesome breakfast. It should contain sufficient calories, carbohydrate, protein, fat and fluid.
- Carry healthy snacks with you which can keep you lively throughout the day.
- Don't miss out on taking water and other fluids.
- Plump for lunch which like breakfast contains macro as well as micronutrients and is not stodgy which may make you too full to travel the rest of the day.
- Select the menu wisely when stopping at a restaurant.
- Additionally you can bring oral nutritional supplements (ONS) so that you can intake calories, carbohydrates, protein and vitamins and

minerals if it is difficult to adapt to the local menu.
- Approach high biological value protein sources like egg, chicken, meat, fish.
- As muscle loss is common in high altitude, protein synthesis should be prioritized. In order to maintain protein mass, key branched chain amino acids like leucine, isoleucine, and valine are recommended to be included in diet.
- High carbohydrate diet should be followed to ward off muscle loss.
- Encourage unsaturated sources of fat like olives, nuts, seeds.

Foods To Include In High Altitude

When venturing into high-altitude environments, proper nutrition becomes a crucial factor in maintaining health, energy, and performance. The unique challenges posed by reduced oxygen levels, increased physical exertion, and extreme weather conditions demand a carefully curated diet. This article explores the essential foods to include in your high-altitude meal plan, ensuring your body receives the necessary nutrients to thrive in these demanding environments.

Healthy Eating Plate

Complex Carbohydrates: The High-Altitude Fuel

At high altitudes, the body relies heavily on carbohydrates for energy. Complex carbohydrates provide sustained energy release, crucial for endurance activities common in mountainous terrain.

Key foods to include

- Whole grain cereals (wheat, pasta and bread or other local grown millets or grains as available)
- Rice of any variety as it boosts up the nergy level quickly.
- Quinoa if available or if can be carried.
- Oatmeal
- Sweet potatoes or potatoes

These foods not only provide energy but also contain important vitamins and minerals. For instance, quinoa offers a complete protein profile, while sweet potatoes are rich in beta-carotene, supporting overall health.

Lean Proteins: Building Blocks for Adaptation

Adequate protein intake is essential for muscle repair and the production of red blood cells, which increases at high altitudes. Recommended protein sources:

- Lean meats (chicken, turkey)
- Fish (locally available fishes, salmon, trout)
- Eggs
- Legumes (lentils, beans or other local grown legumes)
- Low-fat dairy products

Fatty fishes offer the added benefit of omega-3 fatty acids, which may help reduce inflammation and support cardiovascular health during altitude exposure.

Healthy Fats: Concentrated Energy Source

Fats provide a concentrated source of energy and help with the absorption of fat-soluble vitamins.

Ideal fat sources include:

- Nuts (almonds, walnuts) and Oil seeds

- Avocados
- Any oils as locally available or Olive oil, canola oil

These foods also offer additional benefits. For example, walnuts are rich in omega-3 fatty acids, while chia seeds provide fiber and antioxidants.

Iron-Rich Foods: Oxygen Carriers

Iron is crucial for the formation of hemoglobin, which carries oxygen throughout the body. This becomes even more important at high altitudes where oxygen is scarce.

Iron-rich foods to pack:

- Lean red meat
- Spinach and other leafy greens
- Dried fruits (apricots, raisins)
- Fortified cereals

Pairing these with vitamin C-rich foods enhances iron absorption. For instance, having a spinach salad with bell peppers or a small amount of citrus fruit with your meal can boost iron uptake.

Antioxidant-Rich Foods: Combating Oxidative Stress

High altitudes expose the body to increased oxidative stress. Antioxidant-rich foods help combat this stress and support overall health.

Antioxidant powerhouses include:

- Berries (blueberries, strawberries)
- Dark chocolate
- Green tea
- Colorful vegetables (bell peppers, carrots)

Dark chocolate, in particular, not only provides antioxidants but can also help improve blood flow, which is beneficial at high altitudes.

Hydrating Foods: Supporting Fluid Balance

Staying hydrated is crucial at high altitudes, and certain foods can contribute to your overall fluid intake.

Hydrating food options to add in your food basket:
Watermelon, Cucumbers, Celery, Oranges, Soups and broths

These foods not only provide hydration but also essential electrolytes, helping maintain proper fluid balance.

Easily Digestible Foods: Combating Altitude-Related Digestive Issues

It has been studied that, at high altitude due to low oxygen concentration, a person feels more satiety and less hungry or anorexic. At high altitude, the heart rate increases to fulfill the need of oxygen demanded by the organs to acclimatize. Due to increased heart rate the digestive efficiency of food is reduced.

There is a decrease in the amount of blood flowing to digestive organs and increased blood flow to the brain, heart and lungs. In addition, there is a decrease in the core body temperature and reduces the motility of the gastrointestinal muscle which further leads to distension of colon and reduced Gastrointestinal (GI) secretion. At high altitude, there is an alteration of gut hormones such as leptin and cholecystokinin which suppress appetite as well as GI discomfort. Hypobaric hypoxic conditions may cause reduction in the secretion of digestive enzymes & gastric motility which results in slow digestion of food, malabsorption and hence malnutrition.

A person feels anorexic and has a vomiting sensation. It has been studied that, anaerobic bacteria population grows at high altitude regions. Helicobacter pylori are very common & popular bacteria present at high altitude may also be the cause to damage the pyloric lining of the stomach at higher altitude.

The growth of the gut microbiota can be determined by the diet consumed. Dietary habits and the food group consumed significantly impacts the composition of gut microbiota. It has been observed that, a diet rich in prebiotics with high fiber content, as in Vegetarian, Mediterranean and in Fermentable Oligosaccharide Disaccharide, Monosaccharides and Polyols (FODMAP) promotes the growth of healthy intestinal microbiota and hence reducing the consequences of inflammation and disease. The diet affects the internal atmosphere of the gut microbiota. Fermented food contains a good amount of healthy microorganisms as probiotics.Some of the food items that contain probiotics like yogurt, fermented soy product, etc . impart the benefits to the intestinal mucosa and reduce the risk of inflammation and disease.

Additionally high altitudes can sometimes lead to digestive discomfort. Including easily digestible foods can help mitigate these issues. Some of the stomach-friendly options include - Bananas, White rice, Cooked vegetables, Lean, grilled meats, Yogurt (if tolerant to dairy)

Bananas, in particular, offer the added benefit of being rich in potassium, an important electrolyte often lost through increased respiration and perspiration at altitude.

Portable, Nutrient-Dense Snacks

Having quick, easily accessible snacks is crucial for maintaining energy levels during high-altitude activities. Ideal snack options include:

- Trail mix (nuts, seeds, dried fruits)
- Energy bars
- Nut butter packets
- Jerky (beef or plant-based alternatives)
- Dried seaweed snacks (for iodine and minerals)

These snacks provide a good balance of carbohydrates, proteins, and fats, along with essential micronutrients.

Proper nutrition at high altitudes goes beyond merely satisfying hunger. It's about providing your body with the right balance of nutrients to support increased metabolic demands, combat oxidative stress, and maintain overall health in challenging environments. By incorporating these essential foods into your high-altitude diet, one can enhance body's ability to adapt to altitude, improve performance, and enjoy a safer, more comfortable mountain experience.

Remember, individual nutritional needs can vary based on factors such as altitude, duration of stay, physical activity level, and personal health conditions. It's always advisable to consult with a nutritionist or healthcare provider experienced in high-altitude health for personalized dietary recommendations before embarking on your high-altitude adventure. With the right nutritional strategy, you can fuel your body effectively and focus on the incredible experiences that high-altitude environments have to offer.

EIGHT

• 41 •

LOCALLY AVAILABLE FOODS IN HIMALAYAN BELT OF INDIA

The Himalayan belt of India offers a diverse and unique cuisine influenced by the region's climate, geography, and cultural traditions. Here's a concise overview of locally available foods and dishes in this area:

Sources of carbohydrate:

Carbohydrates are crucial at high altitudes as they are the body's primary energy source. They help maintain blood glucose levels and replenish glycogen stores, which is essential for sustained energy in low-oxygen environments.

- Rice, rice flour, wheat flour, ragi flour, barley, bread, lentils, black gram, potato, muesli, granola, pasta, quinoa, millets, noodles, dried fruits like dates, figs, apricots are the major sources available at high altitudes.

Grains, principle source of energy

Food	Benefits	Forms of Consumption
Rice and rice flour	Easy to digest, provides quick energy	Cooked rice, rice cakes, rice porridge
Wheat flour	Sustained energy release	Chapatis, breads, pasta
Ragi flour	Rich in calcium, helps in acclimatization	Roti, porridge, cookies
Barley	High in fiber, aids digestion	Soups, stews, added to breads
Lentils and black gram	Protein-rich carbs, aid in muscle recovery	Dal, soups, added to rice dishes
Potato	Quick energy, rich in potassium	Boiled, mashed, added to stews
Muesli and granola	Convenient, nutrient-dense	As is, with milk or yogurt
Quinoa and millets	Complete protein, high in minerals	Cooked like rice, added to soups
Dried fruits	Concentrated energy, rich in minerals	As is, added to trail mix

Ways you can enjoy your fuel sources - sources of carbohydrates

Sources of protein:

Protein is essential for muscle repair and oxygen transport, both of which are critical at high altitudes.

- Egg, meat locally available from chicken, goat, yak, milk powder, milk, buttermilk, soybean, legumes, nuts, himalayan tofu from black beans, fish (mostly canned).

Food	Benefits	Forms of Consumption
Eggs	Complete protein, easily digestible	Boiled, scrambled, added to dishes
Meat (chicken, goat, yak)	High-quality protein, iron source	Grilled, stewed, added to soups
Milk powder	Convenient source of protein and calcium	Reconstituted, added to drinks or food
Buttermilk	Probiotic, aids digestion	As a drink, added to curries
Soybean	Plant-based complete protein	Tofu, tempeh, added to stews
Nuts	Protein and healthy fats	As is, nut butters, added to dishes
Himalayan tofu	Local protein source, easily digestible	Stir-fried, added to soups
Canned fish	Omega-3 fatty acids, protein	As is, added to salads or sandwiches

Enjoy your Proteins

Pivotal to preserve lean mass

Sources Of Branched Chain Amino Acids (BCAA):
Whole gram, lentils, black gram, chickpeas, chicken, eggs, fish, soybean, almonds, brazil nuts, whole wheat.

Key Benefits of BCAAs at High Altitude:
1. Increase appetite, which can be suppressed at altitude
2. Relieve muscle soreness from increased physical exertion
3. Reduce sense of fatigue, common in low-oxygen environments
4. Prevent muscle wasting due to increased metabolic demands
5. Preserve lean mass, crucial for maintaining strength and endurance

When traveling to high altitudes, it's important to include a variety of these foods in your diet. Focus on easily digestible, nutrient-dense options that can be prepared simply or eaten with minimal preparation. Always ensure proper food safety, especially with perishable items like meat and dairy. Staying well-hydrated and eating frequent, smaller meals can help your body adjust to the increased metabolic demands of high-altitude environments.

NINE

GRAB-AND-GO DRY FOODS FOR HIGH ALTITUDE NUTRITION

When embarking on adventures at high altitudes, proper nutrition becomes crucial for maintaining energy, health, and overall well-being. The challenges posed by elevated environments – such as decreased oxygen levels, increased physical exertion, and potential digestive issues – make it essential to choose snacks and foods wisely.

High altitude environments, typically considered to be 8,000 feet (2,438 meters) above sea level or higher, can significantly impact the human body. These effects may include:

- Increased metabolic rate
- Potential loss of appetite
- Altered digestion
- Greater risk of dehydration
- Increased oxidative stress

To combat these challenges and ensure peak performance, it's important to select foods that are:

- Nutrient-dense
- Easy to digest
- Non-perishable

- Lightweight and portable
- Varied in texture and flavor

The following list of grab-and-go dry foods has been carefully curated to meet these criteria. These snacks not only provide essential nutrients but also offer practical benefits for travelers and adventurers heading to high altitudes. Whether you're planning a mountain trek, a high-elevation road trip, or simply visiting a city at altitude, incorporating these foods into your diet can help you stay energized, healthy, and ready for whatever challenges your journey may bring.

Some snacks are indeed excellent choices for road trips, especially when traveling to high altitude destinations. Let's explore each item in more detail:

1. Brazil Nuts: Rich in selenium, these nuts support thyroid function and boost immunity, which is particularly beneficial at high altitudes where the body may be under stress.

2. Walnuts: Packed with omega-3 fatty acids, walnuts provide essential nutrients for brain health and can help reduce inflammation, which is often increased at higher elevations.

3. Banana: A great source of potassium, bananas help maintain proper muscle and nerve function, which can be affected by the altitude. They also provide quick energy in the form of natural sugars.

4. Almonds: High in vitamin E and magnesium, almonds support heart health and can help combat the increased oxidative stress experienced at high altitudes.

5. Energy Bar: These compact snacks provide a balanced mix of carbohydrates, proteins, and fats, offering sustained energy for long journeys or hikes.

6. Dark Chocolate: Rich in antioxidants, dark chocolate can help protect against the increased free radical damage at high altitudes. It also contains caffeine and theobromine, which can provide a mild energy boost.

7. Carrots: Packed with beta-carotene and other antioxidants, carrots support eye health and boost the immune system, which can be compromised at high altitudes.

8. Strawberries: High in vitamin C, strawberries help absorb iron more efficiently, which is crucial for maintaining proper oxygen levels in the blood – a common concern at high altitudes.

9. Orange Berries: Likely referring to sea buckthorn or other orange-colored berries, these are rich in vitamins and antioxidants that support

overall health and combat altitude-related stress.

10. Apple: A good source of fiber and antioxidants, apples can help maintain digestive health and provide hydration, both important factors when traveling to high altitudes.

11. Roasted Seeds (Chia, flax, sunflower, sesame seeds, etc.): These seeds are nutrient-dense, providing essential fatty acids, proteins, and minerals that support overall health and energy levels.

12. Unsalted Peanuts: A good source of protein and healthy fats, peanuts provide sustained energy without the excess sodium that can contribute to dehydration at high altitudes.

13. Rice Flakes: Easy to digest and a good source of carbohydrates, rice flakes provide quick energy and are gentle on the stomach, which can be sensitive at high altitudes.

14. Protein Bar: Similar to energy bars, protein bars offer a balanced nutritional profile with an emphasis on protein, which is essential for muscle repair and maintenance.

15. Roasted Chana: Also known as roasted chickpeas, this snack is high in protein and fiber, providing sustained energy and supporting digestive health.

16. Sattu: A traditional Indian food made from roasted gram flour, sattu is rich in protein and complex carbohydrates, making it an excellent energy source for high altitude travel.

17. Boiled Eggs: Packed with high-quality protein and essential nutrients, boiled eggs are a versatile and filling snack that can help maintain muscle mass at high altitudes.

18. Muesli: A mix of oats, nuts, and dried fruits, muesli provides a balanced combination of carbohydrates, proteins, and fats for sustained energy release.

19. Roasted Corn: A good source of complex carbohydrates and fiber, roasted corn provides energy and helps maintain digestive health.

20. Bread from Local Market: While not a dry food per se, locally sourced bread can be a good source of carbohydrates and may be fortified with vitamins and minerals that support high altitude nutrition.

Remember to pair these snacks with plenty of water to stay properly hydrated, which is crucial at high altitudes. This diverse selection of foods will help ensure that you maintain proper nutrition and energy levels during your high altitude adventures.

TEN

DOS AND DON'TS FOR MOUNTAIN TRAVEL

This table serves as a helpful guide for maintaining good nutrition and health while traveling in mountainous regions. It's important to note that while these are general guidelines, you should always consider your specific health needs and consult with healthcare professionals or local experts for advice tailored to your particular mountain destination.

DOs	DON'Ts
Drinking bottled water to avoid infectious diarrhea.	Drinking water from non-controllable sources.
Try to peel fruits yourself.	Eating undercooked meat or vegetables.
Consuming whole fruits.	Taking sugar, jaggery excessively (it triggers inflammation in the body).
Selecting steamed, sir fried food items.	Beginning meal with deep fried foods (It can suppress appetite).
Encouraging small meals frequently.	Skipping main meals and snacks.
Distributing protein rich foods equally from morning to night.	Having fruit juices with artificial sweeteners (available in the local market).
Having foods rich in antioxidants and anti-inflammatory properties, for example, nuts, seeds, millets, berries, bananas etc.	Consuming red meat frequently in large quantities.
Buying necessary food staff when you stay near a market.	Eating refined noodles every so often.
Taking some light utensils like bowls, plates, spoons etc.	Ordering fried items chiefly on every meal.
Relying on whole grams or legumes to get branched chain amino acids.	Having too much caffeine (high amount of caffeine will result in dehydration).
Preferring boiled egg over poach or omelet.	

Some Dos and Donts for better hiking experience

ELEVEN

RECOVERY STRATEGIES FOR HIGH-PERFORMANCE ATHLETES AT HIGH ALTITUDE

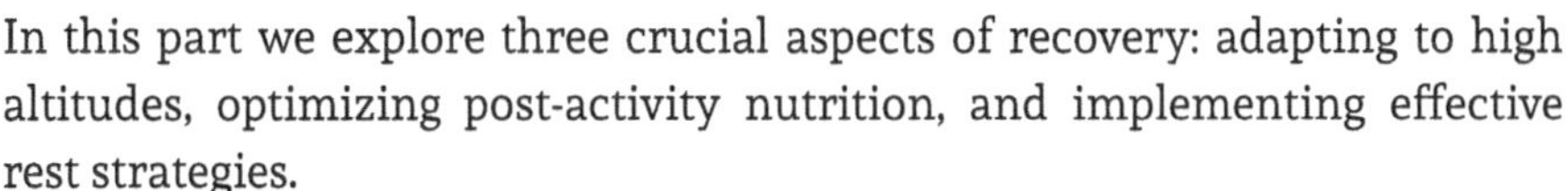

In this part we explore three crucial aspects of recovery: adapting to high altitudes, optimizing post-activity nutrition, and implementing effective rest strategies.

At higher elevations, the partial pressure of oxygen decreases, leading to lower oxygen saturation in the blood. This hypoxic environment triggers a cascade of adaptations in the body:

- Increased red blood cell production: The body compensates for lower oxygen by producing more red blood cells, a process that takes several weeks.
- Enhanced lung capacity: The respiratory rate and depth increase to maximize oxygen intake.
- Improved oxygen utilization: Muscles become more efficient at extracting and using available oxygen.

To support these adaptations:

- Consider a "live high, train low" approach where athletes live at altitude but train at lower elevations to maintain intensity.
- Use pulse oximeters to monitor blood oxygen levels and adjust training loads accordingly.
- Implement altitude tents or simulated altitude environments for pre-acclimatization.

Importance of Post-Activity Nutrition

The "anabolic window" immediately following exercise is a critical period for recovery:

- Glycogen resynthesis: High-intensity exercise depletes muscle glycogen stores. Consuming carbohydrates post-exercise can increase glycogen synthesis rates by up to 50%.
- Protein synthesis: Exercise or climbing creates micro-tears in muscle fibers. Consuming protein provides the amino acids necessary for repair and growth.
- Hormonal environment: Post-exercise, the body is primed for nutrient uptake due to increased insulin sensitivity and elevated levels of growth hormone.

Specific nutritional strategies:

- Aim for 1-1.2g of carbohydrate per kg of body weight within the first hour post-exercise.
- Consume 20-40g of high-quality protein to stimulate muscle protein synthesis.
- Consider adding antioxidant-rich foods to combat exercise-induced oxidative stress.

Rest and Regeneration Strategies

- Recovery is an active process that requires intentional strategies:
- Sleep optimization: Maintain a consistent sleep schedule, even on rest days.
- Create a sleep-conducive environment: dark, cool, and quiet.
- Limit blue light exposure from devices before bedtime.

- Active recovery techniques: Low-intensity cardio can enhance blood flow and reduce muscle soreness.
- Mobility work and stretching can improve flexibility and reduce injury risk.
- Stress management: Cognitive strategies like mindfulness and visualization can reduce mental fatigue.
- Regular psychological check-ins can help identify and address burnout early.
- Recovery technology: Explore tools like percussion therapy devices for targeted muscle recovery.
- Consider pneumatic compression systems to enhance circulation in the limbs.
- Periodization of recovery: Plan recovery days and lower-intensity training periods into the overall training cycle in case of atheletes.
- Implement longer recovery periods (1-2 weeks) between major training blocks or competitions.

By delving deeper into these strategies, one can create comprehensive recovery protocols tailored to individual needs and specific sporting demands. The interplay between altitude adaptation, nutrition, and rest highlights the complexity of athletic recovery and the need for a multifaceted approach to optimize performance and longevity in sport.

End Note

As we conclude our journey through the intricacies of high-altitude nutrition, it's important to reflect on the vital role that proper fueling plays in conquering the challenges presented by elevated environments. Throughout this book, we've explored the unique physiological demands of high-altitude activities and the crucial importance of tailored nutritional strategies.

From understanding the basics of altitude's effects on the human body to delving into specific meal plans and addressing special dietary considerations, we've aimed to equip you with the knowledge necessary for safe and successful high-altitude adventures. Remember that while the information provided here is comprehensive, each individual's needs may vary, and it's always wise to consult with healthcare professionals or nutritionists specializing in high-altitude nutrition before embarking on significant expeditions.

As you prepare for your own high-altitude journeys, whether they be mountain climbing expeditions, high-elevation treks, or extended stays in lofty regions, keep in mind the fundamental principles we've discussed:

1. Proper pre-expedition planning is crucial for success.

2. Balanced nutrition, including appropriate ratios of macronutrients and essential micronutrients, supports your body's increased demands at altitude.

3. Hydration is paramount and requires constant attention in high-altitude environments.

4. Listening to your body and adjusting your nutritional intake accordingly can make the difference between struggle and triumph.

We hope that this guide serves as a valuable resource in your high-altitude endeavors, helping you to fuel your summit aspirations effectively and safely. May your adventures be nourishing in every sense, allowing you to reach new heights both literally and figuratively.

Remember, with the right knowledge and preparation, you can overcome the nutritional challenges of high altitudes and fully embrace the awe-inspiring experiences that await you at the top of the world.

Safe travels and happy climbing!

Glossary

Key Terms and Definitions

Acclimatization: The process by which the body adapts to reduced oxygen levels at high altitudes.

Acute Mountain Sickness (AMS): A common condition experienced at high altitudes, characterized by headache, nausea, fatigue, and dizziness.

Antioxidants: Substances that can prevent or slow damage to cells caused by free radicals, particularly important at high altitudes due to increased oxidative stress.

Basal Metabolic Rate (BMR): The number of calories your body burns at rest, which typically increases at high altitudes.

Carbohydrate Loading: A strategy to maximize the storage of glycogen in the body before high-intensity or endurance activities.

Electrolytes: Minerals in the blood and other bodily fluids that carry an electric charge, crucial for maintaining proper hydration and muscle function.

Glycogen: The stored form of glucose in the body, primarily in the liver and muscles, serving as a readily available energy source.

High Altitude: Generally defined as elevations above 2,400 meters (8,000 feet) where atmospheric pressure is significantly lower than at sea level.

Hydration Status: The state of the body's water balance, crucial to monitor at high altitudes due to increased fluid loss.

Hypoxia: A condition in which the body or a region of the body is deprived of adequate oxygen supply at the tissue level.

Macronutrients: The nutrients required in large amounts in the diet: carbohydrates, proteins, and fats.

Micronutrients: Essential dietary elements required by organisms in small quantities: vitamins and minerals.

Oxidative Stress: An imbalance between free radicals and antioxidants in the body, often increased at high altitudes.

Protein Synthesis: The process by which cells build proteins, which can be affected by high altitude.

Thermic Effect of Food (TEF): The increase in metabolic rate that occurs after ingestion of food.

References

Here are the references arranged in APA format and alphabetical order:

Alasalvar, C., Salvadó, J. S., & Ros, E. (2020). Bioactives and health benefits of nuts and dried fruits. Food Chemistry, 314, 126192. https://doi.org/10.1016/j.foodchem.2020.126192

Beall, C. M. (2007). Two routes to functional adaptation: Tibetan and Andean high-altitude natives. Proceedings of the National Academy of Sciences, 104(Suppl 1), 8655-8660. https://doi.org/10.1073/pnas.0701985104

Berger, J., Muza, S., Swenson, E. R., Fulco, C. S., & Bärtsch, P. (2006). Effect of sex on high-altitude sleep apnea. American Journal of Respiratory and Critical Care Medicine, 174(12), 1264-1267. https://doi.org/10.1164/rccm.200606-826OC

Brutsaert, T. D., Parra, E. J., Shriver, M. D., Gamboa, A., Palacios, J. A., & Rivera, M. (2002). Effects of birthplace and individual genetic admixture on lung volume and exercise phenotypes of Peruvian Quechua. American Journal of Physical Anthropology, 119(1), 4-18. https://doi.org/10.1002/ajpa.10068

George, E. S., Daly, R. M., Tey, S. L., Brown, R., Wong, T. H. T., & Tan, S. Y. (2022). Perspective: Is it Time to Expand Research on "Nuts" to Include "Seeds"? Justifications and Key Considerations. Advances in Nutrition, 13(4), 1016–1027. https://doi.org/10.1093/advances/nmac028

Górska-Warsewicz, H., Laskowski, W., Kulykovets, O., Kudlińska-Chylak, A., Czeczotko, M., & Rejman, K. (2018). Food Products as Sources of Protein and Amino Acids-The Case of Poland. Nutrients, 10(12), 1977. https://doi.org/10.3390/nu10121977

Grocott, M. P., Martin, D. S., Levett, D. Z., McMorrow, R., Windsor, J., & Montgomery, H. E. (2009). Arterial blood gases and oxygen content in climbers on Mount Everest. New England Journal of Medicine, 360(2), 140-149. https://doi.org/10.1056/NEJMoa0801581

Hackett, P. H., & Roach, R. C. (2001). High-altitude illness. New England Journal of Medicine, 345(2), 107-114. https://doi.org/10.1056/NEJM200107123450206

Hashempour-Baltork, F., Torbati, M., Azadmard-Damirchi, S., & Savage, G. P. (2017). Quality properties of puffed corn snacks incorporated with sesame seed powder. Food Science & Nutrition, 6(1), 85–93. https://doi.org/10.1002/fsn3.532

Hoffman, J. R., & Falvo, M. J. (2004). Protein - Which is Best?. Journal of Sports Science & Medicine, 3(3), 118–130.

Juliano, S. A., & Cordero, R. A. (2016). Going where few have gone before: Adaptations of adult and larval mosquitoes to extreme temperatures. Physiological Entomology, 41(3), 187-194. https://doi.org/10.1111/phen.12154

Kayser, B. (1992). Nutrition and High Altitude Exposure. International Journal of Sports Medicine, 13 Suppl 1, S129-32. https://doi.org/10.1055/s-2007-1024616

Parise, I. (n.d.). Traveling safely to places at high altitude – Understanding and preventing altitude illness.

Puglisi, M. J., & Fernandez, M. L. (2022). The Health Benefits of Egg Protein. Nutrients, 14(14), 2904. https://doi.org/10.3390/nu14142904

Robbins, A. M., Kordy, H., & Parra, R. C. (2019). Osteological analysis of human skeletal remains from the high-altitude site of Cerro Alero, Peru. International Journal of Osteoarchaeology, 29(2), 307-316. https://doi.org/10.1002/oa.2786

Rondanelli, M., Nichetti, M., Peroni, G., Faliva, M. A., Naso, M., Gasparri, C., Perna, S., Oberto, L., Di Paolo, E., Riva, A., Petrangolini, G., Guerreschi, G., & Tartara, A. (2021). Where to Find Leucine in Food and How to Feed Elderly With Sarcopenia in Order to Counteract Loss of Muscle Mass: Practical Advice. Frontiers in Nutrition, 7, 622391. https://doi.org/10.3389/fnut.2020.622391

Schena, F., Guerrini, F., Tregnaghi, P., & Kayser, B. (1992). Branched-chain amino acid supplementation during trekking at high altitude. The effects on loss of body mass, body composition, and muscle power. European Journal of Applied Physiology and Occupational Physiology, 65(5), 394–398. https://doi.org/10.1007/BF00243503

Schuler, B., Thomsen, J. J., Gassmann, M., & Lundby, C. (2007). Timing the arrival at 2340 m altitude for aerobic performance. Scandinavian Journal of Medicine & Science in Sports, 17(5), 588-594. https://doi.org/10.1111/j.1600-0838.2006.00618.x

Sierra, J. A., Escobar, J. S., Corrales-Agudelo, V., Lara-Guzmán, O. J., Velásquez-Mejía, E. P., Henao-Rojas, J. C., Caro-Quintero, A., Vaillant, F., & Muñoz-Durango, K. (2022). Consumption of golden berries (Physalis peruviana L.) might reduce biomarkers of oxidative stress and alter gut permeability in men without changing inflammation status or the gut microbiota. Food Research International, 162(Pt A), 111949. https://doi.org/10.1016/j.foodres.2022.111949

Slavin, J., & Carlson, J. (2014). Carbohydrates. Advances in Nutrition, 5(6), 760–761. https://doi.org/10.3945/an.114.006163

Stobdan, T., Akbari, A., Azad, P., Zhou, D., Poulsen, O., Appenzeller, O., ... & Aldashev, A. (2017). EPAS1 gain-of-function mutation contributes to high-altitude adaptation in Tibetan horses. Molecular Biology and Evolution, 34(11), 2947-2958. https://doi.org/10.1093/molbev/msx219

Tschop, M., & Morrison, K. M. (2001). Weight loss at high altitude. Advances in Experimental Medicine and Biology, 502, 91-104. https://doi.org/10.1007/978-1-4757-3401-0_8

Viscor, G., Corominas, J., & Carceller, A. (2023). Nutrition and Hydration for High-Altitude Alpinism: A Narrative Review. International Journal of Environmental Research and Public Health, 20(4), 3186. https://doi.org/10.3390/ijerph20043186

Wallace, T. C., Murray, R., & Zelman, K. M. (2016). The Nutritional Value and Health Benefits of Chickpeas and Hummus. Nutrients, 8(12), 766. https://doi.org/10.3390/nu8120766

Wells, L., Lipschitz, D. A., Klein, R. M., & Thompson, H. (2010). Nutrition and upper extremity performance: A preliminary investigation of New Orleans high school students. Journal of the American Dietetic Association, 78(2), 139-144. https://doi.org/10.1016/0002-8223(81)90208-9

West, J. B. (2017). High-altitude physiology and pathophysiology: Implications and relevance for intensive care medicine. Critical Care, 21(1), 308. https://doi.org/10.1186/s13054-017-1894-5